Rings And Other Things

Wendy Pettingill-Jones

Made with ❤ on the BookLeaf Publishing Platform
www.bookleafpub.in
www.bookleafpub.com

Dedication

To my husband Mardis, *for loving a chaotic woman as far out there as the rings of Saturn.*

Preface

Vulnerability is strength.

This poetry collection, which has been in the making since 2019, is a raw and deeply personal one. While the details are specific to my experiences from the past five years, my hope is that the larger themes resonate with my readers. To anyone who has experienced chronic illness, divorce, trauma, or mental health issues, I hope this collection makes you feel less alone.

Compiling half a decade of experiences into something cohesive has been extremely healing for me. Perhaps, you can find some peace within my words too. Without further ado, I invite you to follow me on a breadcrumb style trail of rings and other things.

All the best, my friends.

Acknowledgements

I have endless gratitude for the members of my monthly writing group. This poetry collection would not be possible without your support and edits.

Kassie Adkins:
My fellow poet and our Queen of Grumpy Old Men Characters.

Caleb Hughes:
Our King of Fantasy and Dialogue.

Emily Tennison:
Our Queen of Descriptions and Cool Character Names.

Kathryn Tennison:
Our fabulous host and Queen of Spook.

Long may we reign!

Love,
Your Queen of Revisions

1. Influences

You shaped me

> like the cages
> put over young
> tomato plants.

2. A Story About Coffee

I spilled my coffee. Specks of grounds swirled
in the small puddle left behind. *No big deal.*
A quick wipe down will do the trick, I shrug.

I forgot to put my coffee cup beneath the Keurig.
Twelve fluid ounces covered the kitchen floor like dirty
lake water. *How unusual for me to forget something so*
simple, I shrug.

My favorite coffee mug slipped from my hands
as I washed the dishes. Water streamed through
the prominent fracture along the handle.
I can't believe I was so clumsy.
I will buy a replacement, I shrug.

My colleague treated me to espresso at a local coffee
shop. I stumble like a drunk out of the car, unable to feel
my legs. *Maybe I was sitting for too long*, I shrug.

My husband asked if I would like coffee
as we waited to see the neurologist.
I declined, having already had three cups before we left.
My heart raced and the smell of cheap roast in the
waiting room made my stomach turn.

We returned to our house and sat in the car
for a long while, not ready to go inside.
When we did, the counter full of mugs
I was too tired to put away stared back at me.
Each of them chipped and clearly still dirty
with tell-tale dark rings at the bottom.

Unbelievable, just how long it took for me to see
The damage that had been under my nose
the whole time.

3. A Sequel About Coffee

It's four years later now
and I think of how the cracked coffee cup
shuddered in my hands
while our home flooded over with all of those feelings
that the 12 ounce volume could no longer contain.
I remember the feeling of steaming coffee spilling
from the holes in my swiss cheese brain.

I think of how dark rings on the counter are no matter
when you can't explain exactly how, or when, or why
you broke the cup, only knowing that you did and how
you hid the fragments as you watched the extra coffee
grounds swirl down the kitchen drain.

It's four years later now
and your last name is nothing but a distant memory.
I wake and wonder if you think of me. I wake and think
of the moment you said, "Oh, everyone will just think I
left my sick wife," and how those words on that bloody
knife laid beside the coffee grounds
as they swirled further and further down.

That was the moment I knew you only cared
about appearances.

Wanting to show off your unbloodied knife
your perfect wife, her trembling hands still holding
perfect unchipped ceramic
And so I picked up the pieces and told myself
that this broken mug filled to its jagged edges
(perhaps only 8 ounces now)
was finally enough.

4. Hesitation

I contemplate the fact that this house is not our home
as I cover the floor with empty boxes
that will soon contain my things
and the lingering scent of a decade of memories.

I smoke a joint to cover the smell. I smoke a cigarette to
cover the smell of the joint. I wash my hands. I shower in
scorching water. I scrub until it feels like I could bleed. I
scrub until I actually bleed. Apply a bandage. Let it heal.

But I'm not ready. I keep moving. I fill the boxes.
But I'm not ready. I haven't healed.

5. She's Little

When my therapist asked me
"What age is the part of you that is hurting?"
All I could say was, "She's little."

I conjured the image of her six-year-old fragile body.
The speckled blue coke bottle glasses
The slightly crooked bangs that her daddy gave her
before he deployed to Kuwait. Her favorite purple shorts
and dinosaur t-shirt. Her uneven, but perfectly white
teeth not yet tainted by years of chain smoking.

I conjured the image of her six-year-old healthy body.
Her working pancreas, years before her daddy cried on
the way to the children's hospital.
Her brain not yet cluttered with spots
that would never heal. Her heart having never been
squeezed and drained in a dirty dorm room.

She curled into my lap, and I held her close.
She curled into my lap, and I told her
"We are going to be okay."

6. By The Sink

He deserved more than a wedding ring
discarded by the sink
lined with the water droplets from where
I washed my hands of him
for the final time.

On occasion, I still think about his
wedding band engraving: *Love is work.*
And in another life,
I think we could have made it work.
    It just wasn't this one.

7. Full Moon Detox

Am I the toxin?
The only woman I think I may have ever actually loved
told me so.

Years have passed
and she has since retracted this statement
but still I contemplated her words as we burnt sage
to cleanse my new home of the negative energy
while charging citrine and smoky quartz in the
moonlight

> I secretly wondered
> if I should be having an allergic reaction.

8. Barton Hollow

Nearly three in the morning: the witching hour
I wait for my nails to dry.

I listen to The Civil Wars
wondering how such a perfect duo split apart.

The most haunting combination of voices
I think I've ever heard.

And when I listen to Joy's new music
I just know that his ghost lingers.

My nails dry and I'm left to sit
and think of what I've lost.

9. Sylvia Plath

Just yesterday I contemplated
with a fellow depressed lady friend
the fact that poets tend to suffer more
from mental illness.

I stared at my electric oven for hours
silently wishing it was gas.

10. Is Your Bed Getting Cold?

Our old queen-size mattress
is in the guest bedroom of my new apartment
I hated it from the moment I first laid on it.

It was likely our most expensive wedding gift
and I didn't want to cause a rift, but I resented that you
asked your brother for a pillow-top
when I'd begged for firmness non-stop.

And now, this perfectly firm king-size
in my master bedroom
eases the pain of my fragile little bones.
But sometimes, despite my best efforts,
I imagine you sleeping in your new bed alone.

In the middle of the night, I crawl to the guest bedroom
when I wake in the morning, a smile crosses my face
because the aching feels familiar
on my fragile little bones.

11. Christmas Cactus (or really, a Thanksgiving Cactus)

I am coming to terms
with the fact that it's alright
         to bloom out of season.

12. In No Particular Order: A List of Things I Want To Say To People No Longer in My Life

I want to show you my new journal. It's olive green. You would love it.

I saw a video that reminded me of you. My finger hovered over the send button for an hour.

I hope your cats are healthy and not stealing all of your Popeye's fried chicken.

I miss your laugh and soft podcast voice.

Every time I see a sea turtle knick-knack I wonder if you got the chance to go to the ocean.

Sometimes, I still carry your crystal with me in my left pocket.

I'm starting to think I was the toxic one. I'm growing though, and I wish you could see it.

I'm so sorry I missed your funeral. I should visit your grave, sometime.

I kept the plant you gave me alive. It likes the morning light in my tiny kitchen.

13. Mistakes on Mara Lynn

Covered in dirt, blood, and the beginnings of bruises
You say it's not my fault.

Beneath the yellow light bulb shining from the patio
I thought he was going to kill you in the parking lot.

The guilt of your black eye and broken nose
and busted head makes me wish
I would have just let him fuck me.

14. The Day After Mistakes Were Made

I went to the store to pick up a new white button-down
None of them looked quite right
when I held them in my trembling hands

And yeah, I probably could have gotten out
your blood stains, but no amount of scrubbing
could have removed the memories.

Dread hit me when I walked
back to my car empty-handed
because I couldn't even pick a basic shirt.

Every man that passes too close
makes me leap out of my own skin now
I will never feel safe in a parking lot again.

15. Ex-Smoker

Much like the cigarette I extinguished on
the railing of your balcony

    The embers of whatever this was,
    fell unceremoniously to the ground below.

16. I Wish I Would Have Gone to New Mexico (Though It Would Have Been a Bad Idea)

For all of my chaos, I couldn't justify it - but
I'm sorry I didn't go with you to dig in the holy sands
at St. Joseph's Stairs

when you spontaneously asked me on a Thursday night.
I think it would have been good for my soul
if I had one left.

17. Emotional Hangover Haiku: Part One

Listening to your
footsteps going down the stairs
hurts worse every time.

18. Emotional Hangover Haiku: Part Two

I want you to stay—
Not just a bit longer but
every single day.

19. Gemini Garden

Your hands crawl up my body
like wandering vines of ivy
clinging intently to the tall wooden fence
I've built around my heart.

Perhaps it's because I'm a Gemini
those chaotic, dueling twins inside me
but I either feel every little thing
or absolutely nothing at all.

Letting your fingertips grow into my wooden splinters
filling cracks between planks with lush green leaves
They have so much higher to climb, but I am unmoving
This fence is worn from the weather; this fence
is my last broken down defense.

I warned you I had walls. I warned you, but somehow it
doesn't seem to bother you at all.
Why aren't you afraid of my chipped off paint?
Afraid of the shadow from the height of the fence
when the sunlight doesn't bounce off it just right?

You continue to sink in deeper, and grow higher
and your touch grows increasingly tender

with each passing day. And the twin that is winning
is the one who feels everything.

20. The Devil is in the Details

The type of love that is devotion
to the smallest of details & those little daily tasks
like taking your laundry back to their place
since you don't have a washer or dryer.
like filling up the ice cube tray since you hate
room temperature water & they want you to drink more
so as not to get dehydrated, like taking out your trash
before they head home, like setting the clock on your
microwave because you aren't sure whether it was your
depression being too relentless to let you lift your finger
to press the buttons or if it was your scatterbrain that
made you forget,
again.

The type of love that convinces you that the entirety of
the cosmos fits inside another person. Or honestly, just
within their eyes. the tiny flecks of galaxy-in-iris, the
space-time continuum in the crinkles when they smile.
The flash of a million burning supernovas, such fire that
you could never long for another heat again.

The type of love that is collapsing in their arms
after good sex or a good cry and knowing that even if

you don't deserve it, they will hold you tighter & make
you feel safer than you could have ever dreamed was
possible.

The type of love where the devil comes
He taps you on your shoulder & whispers
all the awful ways you could destroy it in an instant.
Benzos in the pocket of your laundry, empty beer bottles
rattling as they carry out the trash, random bouts of
sobbing & panic attacks that disturb your sweet
universe's sleep. You see the faintest hint of
a solar storm in their eyes as they wake & you wonder
what they could possibly be thinking
but are too afraid to ask.

The type of love that is devotion
to the smallest of details.
The type of love that makes you pray
that you are strong enough to tell the devil to fuck off.

21. Graveyards

He says I leave graveyards in my wake.
My lover smiles softly like the dirt of the earth
as he details every haphazard happening
he can remember from our home.

cups and cans
socks and shoes
shower droplets and wet hair strands
stray damp towels
strung and flung all about.

He says I leave graveyards
in my wake. Single moments engraved
upon mossy gray stones
epitaph lines, tiny trails
of the life I left behind.

I used to think this was
a bad thing. Tiny trails
of rings and other things.
Instead, my lover smiles
toothily like bones in a grave
He tells me confidently
that death never scared him anyway.